GW00382652

HARDY'S NAME	REAL NAME	HARDY'S NAME	REAL NAME
Abbott's Cernel	Cerne Abbas	Longpuddle	
Abbotsea	Abbotsbury	Lornton	Hornton
Aldbrickham	Reading	Lulwind Cove	Lulworth Cove
Alderworth	Briantspuddle	Lumsden	Cumnor
Alfredston	Wantage		
Anglebury	Wareham	Markton	Dunster
Arrowthorne	Minstead	Marlbury	Marlborough
Athelhall	Athelhampton	Marlott	Marnhull
		Marshwood	Middlemarsh
Broad Sidlinch	Sidling St. Nicholas	Marygreen	Fawley
Budmouth Regis	Weymouth	Melchester	Salisbury
Bulbarrow	A hill near Sturminster	Mellstock	Stinsford/Bockhampton
	Newton	Melport	Weymouth
		Middleton Abbey	Milton Abbas
Camelton	Camelford	Montislope	Montacute
Carriford	Stinsford/Bockhampton	Moreford	Moreton
Casterbridge	Dorchester		
Castle Boterel	Boscastle	Narroborne	West Coker
Chalk-Newton	Maiden Newton	Nether Moynton	Overmoigne
Charmley	Charminster	Newland Buckton	Buckland Newton
Chaseborough	Cranbourne	Norcombe Hill	A hill near Toller Down
Chene Manor	Canford Magna	Nuttlebury	Hazelbury Bryan
Christminster	Oxford		
Cliff Martin	Coombe Martin	Oakbury Fitzpiers	Okeford Fitzpaine
Clyfton Horseleigh	Clifton Maybank	Oozewood	Ringwood
Corvsgate	Corfe Castle	Overcombe	Sutton Poyntz
Cresscombe	Letcombe Basset	Owlscombe	Batcombe
Creston	Preston	Oxwell	Poxwell
Damer's Wood	Came Wood near	Pen-zephyr	Penzance
	Dorchester	Port Bredy	Bridport
Delborough	East Chelborough	Po'sham	Portesham
Dogbury	A hill near High Stoy		
Downstaple	Barnstaple	Redrutin	Redruth
Durnover	Fordington	Ringsworth	Ringstead
		Rookington	Hurn
East Egdon	Affpuddle	Roy-Town	Troytown
East Endelstow	Lesnewth		
Egdon Heath	A composite of the heaths	St. Launces	Launceston
	between Bournemouth	St. Maria's	St. Mary's, Isles of Scilly
	and Dorchester	Sandbourne	Bournemouth
Elm Cranlynch	Corfe Mullen	Scrimpton	Frampton
Emminster	Beaminster	Shadwater	Woodsford
Evershead	Evershot	Shaston	Shaftesbury
Exonbury	Exeter	Sherton Abbas	Sherborne
		Shottsford Forum	Blandford Forum
Fensworth	Letcombe Regis	Silverthorne	Up Exe
Flintcomb-Ash	Plush	Sleeping Green	Carhampton or
Flychett	Lytchett Minster		Withycombe
Fountall	Wells	Solentsea	Southsea
Froom-Everard	West Stafford	Springham	Warmwell
		Stagfoot Lane	Hartfoot Lane:
Gaymead	Shinfield		Melcombe Bingham
Giant's Town	High Town, Isles of Scilly	Stapleford	Stalbridge
Great Hintock	Melbury Bubb/Minterne	Stickleford	Tincleton
	Magna	Stoke Barehills	Basingstoke
		Stourcastle	Sturminster Newton
Havenspool	Poole	Street of Wells	Fortuneswell
Holmstoke	East Stoke/East Holme		
	/West Holme	Tivworthy	Tiverton
		Tolchurch	Tolpuddle
Idmouth	Sidmouth	Tollamore	Stinsford/Bockhampton
Isle of Slingers	Portland	Toneborough	Taunton
Isles of Lyonesse	Isles of Scilly	Tor-upon-Sea	Torquay
Ivell	Yeovil	Trantridge	Pentridge
		Trufal	Truro
Kennetbridge	Newbury		
Kingsbere-sub-Greenhill	Bere Regis	Warborne	Wimborne Minster
Kingscreech	Creech	Weatherbury	Puddletown
King's Hintock	Melbury Osmund	Welland	Charborough
Knapwater	Kingsbury Maurward	Wellbridge	Woolbridge
Knollingwood	Wimbourne St. Giles	West Endelstow	St. Juliot
Knollsea	Swanage	Weyden Priors	Weyhill
		Wherryhorne	Winterborne Came
Leddenton	Gillingham	Wintoncester	Winchester
Lew Everard	West Stafford	Wyndway	Upton
Little Enckworth	Kingston		
Little Hintock	Stockwood/Hermitage	Yalbury Wood	Yellowham Wood

Hardy's mother lived until after he had written his last novel and almost all his stories. She was always a very significant influence on all his published works.

After the Last Breath

There's no more to be done, or feared, or hoped;
None now need watch, speak low, and list, and tire;
No irksome crease outsmoothed, no pillow-slope
Does she require.

Blankly we gaze. We are free to go or stay;
Our morrow's anxious plans have missed their aim;
Whether we leave to-night or wait till day
Counts as the same.

The lettered vessels of medicaments
Seem asking wherefore we have set them here;
Each palliative its silly face presents
As useless gear.

And yet we feel that something savours well;
We note a numb relief withheld before;
Our well-beloved is prisoner in the cell
Of Time no more.

We see by littles now the deft achievement
Whereby she has escaped the wrongers all.
In view of which our momentary bereavement
Outshapes but small.

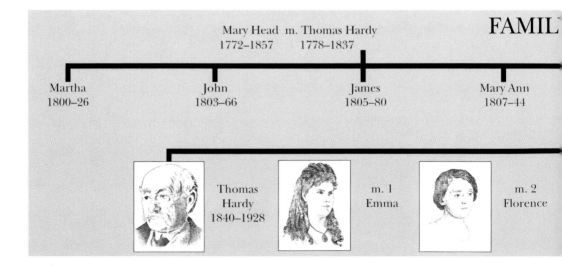

FAMIL

Mary Head m. Thomas Hardy
1772–1857   1778–1837

Martha
1800–26

John
1803–66

James
1805–80

Mary Ann
1807–44

Thomas
Hardy
1840–1928

m. 1
Emma

m. 2
Florence

Thomas Hardy, son of a rustic Dorset builder, was to become an architect, poet, novelist, playwright and essayist. In short, he was a genius, a fact made all the more surprising by his unpromising start in life.

NOTE: *Prose extracts in Hardy's own words appear in italic type.*

Born 2 June 1840, at Higher Bockhampton, near Dorchester, *the smallest and feeblest of folk there,* he was a sickly child, not expected to live past his first years. His childhood, however, was dominated by the rural, domestic events that he would later recall in his poetry, novels and short stories and by the tale-telling and gossip of his elders, and by games and rambles. All of these provided the conditions that Hardy saw as necessary to give meaning to life in an isolated place. He describes them in detail in *The Woodlanders.*

They are old associations – an almost exhaustive biographical or historical acquaintance with every object, animate or inanimate, within the observer's horizon. He must know all about those invisible ones of the days gone by, whose feet have traversed the fields which look so grey from his windows; recall whose creaking plough has turned those sods from time to time; whose hands planted the trees that form a crest to the opposite hill; whose horses and hounds have torn through that underwood; what birds affect that particular brake; what bygone dramas of love, jealousy, revenge, or disappointment have been enacted in the cottages, the mansion, the street or on the green.

In this short book we try to give some insight into the importance of Wessex to Thomas Hardy, particularly in his most well-known novels.

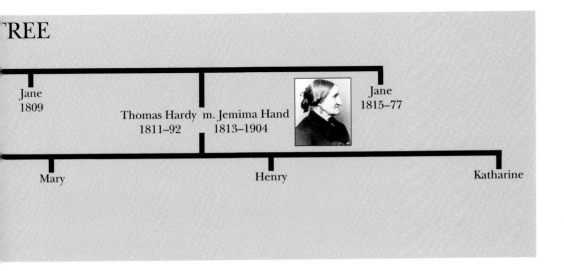

REE

Jane
1809

Thomas Hardy m. Jemima Hand
1811–92   1813–1904

Jane
1815–77

Mary

Henry

Katharine

The Hardy family home had been built by Thomas's great-grandfather, Thomas the First, for his son, Thomas the Second. 'Standing alone, mud walls and thatched' as an insurance policy of 1829 described it, the cottage was unusual for the time because it was inhabited by a single family – Thomas Hardy (the Second), his wife Jemima, and their four children of whom the oldest, Thomas, was to immortalise it.

It stood in a spot remote enough for it to be used as a smuggler's store for brandy landed between Weymouth and Lulworth Cove. Egdon Heath lay to the east, a vast and wild territory which played a prominent part in *The Return of the Native* in particular.

The garden was large enough for the cultivation of vegetables, apples (gathered for the cider-maker with his *mill, and tubs, and vat, and press*), a pig for killing and salting each autumn, beehives for honey and sometimes, for carrying heavy goods, a horse.

Birthplace of Thomas Hardy at Higher Beckhampton, near Dorchester. From this isolated cottage his career as an architect began; it lasted until 1872, when the success of Under the Greenwood Tree *persuaded Hardy to pursue a writer's career.*

The Ghost of the Past

We two kept house, the Past and I,
    The Past and I;
Through all my tasks it hovered nigh,
    Leaving me never alone.
It was a spectral housekeeping
    Where fell no jarring tone,
As strange, as still a housekeeping
    As ever has been known.

As daily I went up the stair
    And down the stair,
I did not mind the Bygone there –
    The Present once to me;
Its moving meek companionship
    I wished might ever be,
There was in that companionship
    Something of ecstasy.

It dwelt with me just as it was,
    Just as it was
When first its prospects gave me pause
    In wayward wanderings,
Before the years had torn old troths
    As they tear all sweet things,
Before gaunt griefs had torn old troths
    And dulled old rapturings.

And then its form began to fade,
    Began to fade,
Its gentle echoes faintlier played
    At eves upon my ear
Than when the autumn's look embrowned
    The lonely chambers here,
When autumn's setting shades embrowned
    Nooks that it haunted near.

And so with time my vision less,
    Yea, less and less
Makes of that Past my housemistress,
    It dwindles in my eye;
It looms a far-off skeleton
    And not a comrade nigh,
A fitful far-off skeleton
    Dimming as days draw by.

Thomas Hardy (the writer) played the violin and accordion. 'The Dorchester Hornpipe' was found in a music book of his.

The Choirmaster's Burial

The choirmaster here referred to was Thomas Hardy I, the poet's grandfather. He was the founder of the village choir at Stinsford church; the sketch shows the interior at that time. Thomas Hardy II, the poets father, was the 'tenor man'.

He often would ask us
That, when he died,
After playing so many
To their last rest,
If out of us any
Should here abide.
And it would not task us,
We would with our lutes
Play over him
By his grave-brim
The psalm he liked best –
The one whose sense suits
'Mount Ephraim' –
And perhaps we should seem
To him, in Death's dream,
Like the seraphim.

As soon as I knew
That his spirit was gone
I thought that his due,
And spoke thereupon.
'I think,' said the vicar,
'A read service quicker
Than viols out-of-doors
In these frosts and hoars.
That old-fashioned way

Requires a fine day,
And it seems to me
It had better not be.'

Hence, that afternoon,
Though never knew he
That his wish could not be,
To get through it faster
They buried the master
Without any tune.

But 'twas said that, when
At the dead of next night
The vicar looked out,
There struck on his ken
Thronged roundabout,
Where the frost was graying
The headstoned grass,
A band all in white
Like the saints in church-glass,
Singing and playing
The ancient stave
By the choirmaster's grave.

Such the tenor man told
When he had grown old.

Music was important – both his father and grandfather were members of the Stinsford church choir, near Bockhampton. Hardy the writer also sang in the choir, which in those days was accompanied by viola and not the 'new-fangled' organ of later days. He was to recall these musical experiences through the members of the Mellstock quire in *Under the Greenwood Tree*.

During Hardy's childhood the labourer was always on the edge of pauperism and women like Tess (of the d'Urbervilles) would often have to be employed, as she was, on threshing machines and at such heavy tasks as swede-hacking.

The swede-field in which she and her companion were set hacking was a stretch of a hundred odd acres, in one patch, on the highest ground of the farm, rising above stony lanchets or lynchets – the outcrop of siliceous veins in the chalk formation, composed of myriads of loose white flints in bulbous, cusped, and phallic shapes. The upper half of each turnip had been eaten off by the live-stock, amd it was the business of the two women to grub up the lower or earthy half of the root with a hooked fork called a hacker, that it might be eaten also. ...In the afternoon the rain came on again.

...There are degrees of dampness, and a very little is called being wet through in common talk. But to stand working slowly in a field, and feel the creep of rain-water, first in legs and shoulders, then on hips and head, then at back, front, and sides, and yet to work on till the leaden light diminishes and marks that the sun is down, demands a distinct modicum of stoicism, even of valour.

Stinsford church at the time when Thomas Hardy II, the poet's father, was the 'tenor man'.

The Reverend Charles Kegan Paul wrote, as late as 1868, that 'Wages are so low that a man with children above eight years old is glad of the few shillings which may be earned by them, and the employers of labour insist on these boys being sent into the fields, even if the parents would willingly make an effort to keep them at school. The farmer finds it pays him well to get two boys who, under a man, will do a man's work, but whose combined work costs less than an able-bodied man's wages.'

Lulworth Cove, the scene on the Dorset coast of Frank Troy's supposed disappearance.

Hardy's architectural career lasted from the time he left school in 1856 until 1872. This quiet, small, but no longer delicate young man, fell in love with Emma Lavinia Gifford. Their wedding took place in London, on 17 September, at St. Peter's Church, Paddington, largely because of the hostility between the respective families. The only existing reference by Hardy to the ceremony is in the marriages column of the *Dorset County Chronicle*, 24 September 1874, as given above. The tension between Hardy's mother, who exerted a strong influence over him, and Emma, whom he had met when he was a young architect in St. Juliot, Cornwall, never abated and, in many ways, Jemima Hardy provided food for her son's writing.

Far from the Madding Crowd was Hardy's first published novel after his marriage.

… *'I am perfectly convinced that he is still alive.'*

Bathsheba remained firm in this opinion till Monday, when two circumstances conjoined to shake it. The first was a short paragraph in the local newspaper, which, beyond making by a methodizing pen formidable presumptive evidence of Troy's death by drowning, contained the important testimony of a young Mr. Barker, M.D., of Budmouth, who spoke of being an eyewitness of the accident, in a letter to the editor. In this he stated that he was passing over the cliff on the remoter side of the cove just as the sun was setting. At that time he saw a bather carried along in the current outside the mouth of the cove, and guessed in an instant that there was but a poor chance for him unless he should be possessed of unusual muscular powers. He drifted behind a projection of the coast, and Mr. Barker followed along the shore in the same direction. But by the time that he could reach an elevation sufficiently great to command a view of the sea beyond, dusk had set in, and nothing further was to be seen.

The other circumstance was the arrival of his clothes…

The King's Arms Hotel, Dorchester, was the old coaching inn into which Boldwood carried Bathsheba, who had fainted on being told of the death of her husband.

He entered the gravel path which would take him behind the tower. The path, instead of being stony as it had been the night before, was browned over with a thin coating of mud. At one place in the path he saw a tuft of stringy roots washed white and clean as a bundle of tendons. He picked it up – surely it could not be one of the primroses he had planted? He saw a bulb, another, and another as he advanced. Beyond doubt they were the crocuses. With a face of perplexed dismay Troy turned the corner and then beheld the wreck the stream had made.

The pool upon the grave had soaked away into the ground, and in its place was a hollow. The disturbed earth was washed over the

grass and pathway in the guise of the brown mud he had already seen, and it spotted the marble tombstone with the same stains. Nearly all the flowers were washed clean out of the ground, and they lay, roots upwards, on the spots whither they had been splashed by the stream....

He slowly withdrew from the grave. He did not attempt to fill up the hole, replace the flowers, or do anything at all. He simply threw up his cards and forswore his game for that time and always. Going out of the churchyard silently and unobserved – none of the villagers having yet risen – he passed down some fields at the back, and emerged just as secretly upon the high road. Shortly afterwards he had gone from the village.

It was in the churchyard of Puddletown Church that Frank Troy planted flowers on the grave of Fanny Robin, only to find that the rain would cruelly wash them away. After this, he had no desire to return to his old life with Bathsheba.

Thomas Hardy lived in many places between his childhood in Higher Bockhampton (1840–56), irregular and sometimes lengthy visits there (1856–74), and his last home, Max Gate (1885–1928), which he designed and had built for him. He and Emma spent two happy years in Riverside Villa, Sturminster Newton, during the early part of their marriage. At this time, Hardy wrote *The Return of the Native*.

He walked along towards home without attending to paths. If anyone knew the heath well it was Clym. He was permneated with its scenes, with its substance, and with its odours. He might be said to be its product. His eyes had first opened thereon; with its appearance all the first images of his memory were mingled; his estimate of life had been coloured by it; his toys had been the flint knives and arrow heads which he found there, wondering why stones should 'grow' to such odd shapes; his flowers, the purple bells and yellow furze; his animal kingdom, the snakes and croppers; his society, its human haunters. Take all the varying hates felt by Eustacia Vye towards the heath, and translate them into loves, and you have the heart of Clym. He gazed upon the wide prospect as he walked, and was glad.

To many persons this Egdon was a place which had slipped out of its century generations ago, to intrude as an uncouth object into this. It was an obsolete thing and few cared to study it.

Egdon Heath covered a vast tract of Dorset. Six years before Hardy's birth, the Tolpuddle martyrs had been sentenced to transportation for attempting to organise a primitive agricultural trade union just a few miles across the heath from Bockhampton. Dorset was described in a guidebook of 1856 as 'a bleak county of chalk downs and sandy heaths, thinly peopled, and below the average of the English counties in fertility', although it had 'a certain charm in its very wildness and the forlorn aspect of its villages'. Hardy's description of it seems to bear this out.

Hardy was a frequent visitor to the new Dorset Museum in Dorchester (the building just beyond the awning) after his move back to the town in 1883. He spent many hours in the library, writing The Mayor of Casterbridge. *(Casterbridge was Hardy's name for Dorchester).*

The years 1878–83 were passed in Tooting, London, and Wimborne, interspersed with holidays in Dorset, Normandy and Cambridge. Thomas and Emma did not find life anywhere so satisfactory as in Dorset, so in June 1883 they returned to Dorchester.

On the first day of 1884 the Dorset County Museum opened the doors to the premises it occupies still. Hardy immediately became a frequent visitor to the handsome reading room with its daily supply of London newspapers and numerous works on historical, philosophical topics. He was already a member of the Dorset Natural History and Antiquarian Field Club (the great Iron Age hill fort, Maiden Castle, and other archaeological sites feature in his works), and by June 1884 had been appointed a local magistrate. Also at this time Hardy began to write *The Mayor of Casterbridge.*

A few score yards brought them to the spot where the town band was now shaking the window-panes with the strains of "The Roast Beef of Old England."

The building before whose doors they had pitched their music-stands was the chief hotel in Casterbridge – namely, the King's Arms. A spacious bow-window projected into the street over the main portico, and from the open sashes came the babble of voices, the jingle of glasses, and the drawing of corks.

. . . That's Mr. Henchard, the Mayor, at the end of the table, a facing ye;'

A friend of Hardy's recorded that '*The Mayor of Casterbridge* was the only tragedy that made [Hardy] weep while writing it.' It is a book centred on one man who is undermined by guilt for his actions as a young man. Being 'strong, ignorant and energetic,' he regrets at twenty-one the marriage he made at eighteen, and in a fit of drunken anger he sells his wife and child for 5 guineas at a county fair to an appreciative sailor. 'Hardy's portrait of Henchard – depressive, black-tempered, self-destructive and also lovable, as a child is lovable – is one of his strongest achievements' (Claire Tomalin, 2006).

Hardy told a friend in a letter of 1887, 'As to despondency I have known the very depths of it – you would be quite shocked if I were to tell you how many weeks and months in bygone years I have gone to bed wishing never to see daylight again.' . . . 'this blackest state of mind' was something he suffered from rarely now, but it sometimes returned.

In 1885 after finishing *The Mayor of Casterbridge* he was "in a fit of depression, as if enveloped in a leaden cloud . . . a tragedy exhibits a state of things in the life of an individual which unavoidably causes some natural aim or desire of his to end in catastrophe when carried out."

. . . "This evening the end of the old year 1885 finds me sadder than many previous New Year's Eves have done."

This was just before the book was published. A reader at Smith, Elder (Hardy's publisher) complained that the 'lack of gentry among the characters made it uninteresting'. Only 750 copies were printed and the book was remaindered in under a year.

William Barnes, 'the Dorset Poet', had preceded Thomas Hardy, on whom he had a strong influence through his poetry and life, as a member of the Dorset County Museum. Barnes had held the post of Honorary Secretary from 1846–58 and was an accomplished engraver.

The Dorset County Museum was founded in 1845 to save the geology, wildlife and history of a county under threat from the newly developing railway network. Over the following years the Museum's collections grew, and in 1928, the year of the death of the County's most famous son, Thomas Hardy, writers of Dorset, such as William Barnes, Thomas Hardy, John Fowles, T.E. Lawrence and Cooper Page are featured in the display cabinets. The fossils of Lyme Regis are on display and the Roman remains of Dorset villas can be walked on.

By 1884 Thomas Hardy had been appointed a local magistrate and had begun to write *The Mayor of Casterbridge*.

This is Hardy's study, as it was in Max Gate, the house he built for himself.

Soon after finishing *The Mayor of Casterbridge*, Hardy was at work on another novel, *The Woodlanders*, which he finished early in 1887.

Hardy made his most important house removal – to Max Gate, Wareham Road, Dorchester – on 29 June 1885 and, five months later, began writing *The Woodlanders*. After it was published in 1887 it attracted enthusiastic reviews. Hardy himself preferred its story to any other of his novels. Perhaps this was because it drew heavily on memories of his mother's talk and the qualities he had admired in his father, which found expression in the character of Giles Winterborne.

The village of Okeford Fitzpaine around the turn of the century. This is one of the three Okeford villages immortalized by the village of Oakbury-Fitzpiers, *in* The Woodlanders.

Winterborne was standing in front of the brick oven in his shirt sleeves, tossing in thorn-sprays, and stirring about the blazing mass with a long-handled, three-pronged Beelzebub kind of fork, the heat shining out upon his streaming face and making his eyes like furnaces; the thorns crackling and sputtering; while Creedle, having ranged the pastry dishes in a row on the table till the oven should be ready, was pressing out the crust of a final apple-pie with a rolling-pin. A great pot boiled on the fire; and through the open door of the back-kitchen a boy was seen seated on the fender, emptying the snuffers and scouring the candlesticks, a row of the latter standing upside down on the hob to melt out the grease.

Two word-pictures from The Woodlanders *describing different aspects of rural life.*

Max Gate, the house that Hardy designed and had built, looking much as it did when he and Emma moved into it.

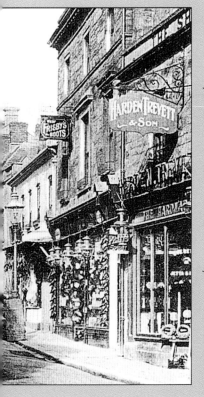

The horses wore their bells that day. There were sixteen to the team, carried on a frame above each animal's shoulders, and tuned to scale, so as to form two octaves, running from the highest note on the right or off-side of the leader to the lowest on the left or near-side of the shaft-horse. Melbury was among the last to retain horse-bells in that neighbourhood; for living at Little Hintock, where the lanes yet remained as narrow as before the days of turnpike roads, these sound-signals were still as useful to him and his neighbours as they had ever been in former times. Much backing was saved in the course of a year by the warning notes they cast ahead; moreover, the tones of all the teams in the district being known to the carters of each, they could tell a long way off on a dark night whether they were about to encounter friends or strangers.

Cheap Street is Sherborne's principal shopping street, and it was in Sheep Street *that Grace met Giles in* The Woodlanders.

Sherborne Abbey. Grace and Giles enter the abbey church at Sherton Abbas.

A fine 16th-century bridge over the Frome adjoins Woolbridge Manor House, which once belonged to a branch of the Turberville family. After their marriage Tess and Angel stay at Wellbridge *in an old farmhouse by a* great Elizabethan bridge.

Hardy's next full-length novel was *Tess of the d'Urbervilles.* The character of Tess was largely formed through memories of past (including childhood) experiences. Many of the events, too, were drawn from childhood associations, but as was his normal custom when working on a novel, the landscape within which the book was set was not re-visited by Hardy during his writing.

The Oxen

In this poem, written in 1915, the 'lonely barton by yonder coomb' was built by Hardy's father.

Christmas Eve, and twelve of the clock.
  'Now they are all on their knees,'
An elder said as we sat in a flock
  By the embers in hearthside ease.

We pictured the meek mild creatures where
  They dwelt in their strawy pen,
Nor did it occur to one of us there
  To doubt they were kneeling then.

So fair a fancy few would weave
  In these years! Yet, I feel,
If someone said on Christmas Eve,
  'Come; see the oxen kneel.

'In the lonely barton by yonder coomb
  Our childhood used to know,'
I should go with him in the gloom,
  Hoping it might be so.

Tess's Lament

I

I would that folk forgot me quite,
    Forgot me quite!
I would that I could shrink from sight.
    And no more see the sun.
Would it were time to say farewell,
To claim my nook, to need my knell,
Time for them all to stand and tell
    Of my day's work as done.

II

Ah! dairy where I lived so long,
    I lived so long;
Where I would rise up staunch and
strong,
    And lie down hopefully.
'Twas there within the chimney-seat
He watched me to the clock's slow beat –
Loved me, and learnt to call me Sweet,
    And whispered words to me.

III

And now he's gone; and now he's
gone;…
    And now he's gone!
The flowers we potted perhaps are
thrown
    To rot upon the farm.
And where we had our supper-fire
May now grow nettle, dock, and briar,
And all the place be mould and mire
    So cozy once and warm.

IV

And it was I who did it all.
    Who did it all:
'Twas I who made the blow to fall
    On him who thought no guile.
Well, it is finished – past, and he
Has left me to my misery,
And I must take my Cross on me
    For wronging him awhile.

V

How gay we looked that day we wed,
    That day we wed!
'May joy be with ye!' they all said
    A-standing by the durn.
I wonder what they say o' us now,
And if they know my lot; and how
She feels who milks my favourite cow,
    And takes my place at churn!

VI

It wears me out to think of it,
    To think of it;
I cannot bear my fate as writ,
    I'd have my life unbe:
Would turn my memory to a blot,
Make every relic of me rot,
My doings be as they were not,
    And gone all trace of me!

On 21 May 1877 Hardy attended an event similar to the Club-day celebration when Tess first saw Angel Clare. About 25 years later this photograph was taken at such a gathering.

Shaftesbury, Shaston, *features in* Tess of the d'Urbervilles, *because Tess goes there to board a carrier's cart to Trantridge so that she can work for the Stoke d'Urbervilles, and in* Jude the Obscure, *Jude enters on the* summit of the peak after a toilsome climb; *Sue and Richard Phillotson's school buildings in Bimport Street* were extensive and stone-built; *whilst waiting for lessons to finish,* Jude withdrew a few steps along Abbey Walk…[then] walked down to the level terrace where the Abbey gardens once had spread *and later on missed his coach which had left from* The Duke's Arms, *The Grosvenor Hotel. Whilst waiting for another, he walked through the* venerable graveyard of Trinity Church, with its avenues of limes *(now the Trinity Centre).*

Christminster, Oxford.

The last of Hardy's novels, and his most socially conscious, *Jude the Obscure,* was written in 1893–94. Although *The Well-Beloved* did not appear until 1897, it had been written ten years earlier.

Jude the Obscure was first published in serial form and the publishers, because they could print 'nothing which could not be read aloud in any family circle', were constrained to alter it quite drastically. Later, when published in its complete form in November 1985, Hardy was 'unprepared for the depth, extent, and directness of the hostility which marked many of the reviews'. The *Guardian* described it as 'a shameful nightmare which one only wishes to forget as quickly and as completely as possible'. The critic, Edmund Gosse, wrote 'It is very gloomy, it is even a grimy, story that Mr. Hardy has at last presented to his admirers . . .' Hardy replied,

The 'grimy' features of the story go to show the contrast between the ideal life a man wished to lead, and the squalid real life he was fated to lead. . . It is, in fact, to be discovered in every body's life.

He now paused at the top of a crooked and gentle declivity, and obtained his first near view of the city. Grey stoned and dun-roofed, it stood within hail of the Wessex border, and almost with the tip of one small toe within it, at the northern-most point of the crinkled line along which the leisurely Thames strokes the fields of that ancient kingdom. The buildings now lay quiet in the sunset, a vane here and there on their many spires and domes giving sparkle to a picture of sober secondary and tertiary hues.

A Cathedral Façade at Midnight

Along the sculptures of the western wall
    I watched the moonlight creeping;
It moved as if it hardly moved at all.
    Inch by inch thinly peeping
Round on the pious figures of freestone, brought
And poised there when the Universe was wrought
To serve its centre, Earth, in mankind's thought.

The lunar look skimmed scantly toe, breast, arm,
    Then edged on slowly, slightly,
To shoulder, hand, face; till each austere form
    Was blanched its whole length brightly
Of prophet, king, queen, cardinal in state,
That dead men's tools had striven to simulate;
And the stiff images stood irradiate.

A frail moan from the martyred saints there set
    Mid others of the erection
Against the breeze, seemed sighings of regret
    At the ancient faith's rejection
Under the sure, unhasting, steady stress
Of Reason's movement, making meaningless
The coded creeds of old-time godliness.

Hardy visited Salisbury in 1860, probably to accompany his sister Mary on her admission to Salisbury Training College (in the King's House in the Close, which now houses the Salisbury and South Wiltshire Museum) and on a holiday in 1897. The pleasure he felt in the peacefulness of the Close is reflected in the poem printed here.

Jude, like Hardy, was a stonemason and he moved to Melchester, Salisbury, hoping to get work on the restoration of the cathedral. Christopher Julian in The Hand of Ethelberta, *published in 1876, is the cathedral organist, and the city is mentioned in several other of Hardy's stories, notably 'On the Western Circuit' (1891) and 'A Committee Man of "The Terror"' (1896).*

The King's House was a familiar place to Hardy's family.

Hardy wrote very little more until after the sudden nd unexpected death of Emma, his first wife, in 1912. Many of his poems refer nostalgically to the time of their courtship; they were written in his later years.

His second wife, Florence, whom he married in 1914, looked after him until his death on 11 January 1928. His ashes are laid in Poets' Corner, Westminster Abbey, but his heart is buried in Emma's grave at Stinsford, next to the tombs of his parents.

Postscript

The story of Tess, even more than that of Jude, seems to show with haunting certainty 'the sheer irrevocability of moments of decision and choice – the opportunity lost, the word unuttered, the road not taken, the beloved recognized or reclaimed too late. It is upon such moments, explored in all their irony and despair, that so many of [Hardy's] novels and stories turn, and some of the most poignant of his personal poems. Almost always it is a woman who pays' (Millgate, 1982).

Feeling sideways they encountered another tower-like pillar, square and uncompromising as the first; beyond it another and another. The place was all doors and pillars, some connected above by continuous architraves.

'A very Temple of the Winds,' he said.

The next pillar was isolated; others composed a trilithon; others were prostrate, their flanks forming a causeway wide enough for a carriage; and it was soon obvious that they made up a forest of monoliths grouped upon the grassy expanse of the plain. The couple advanced further into this pavilion of the night till they stood in its midst.

'It is Stonehenge!' said Clare.

'The heathen temple, you mean?'

Not long after this episode at Stonehenge, in which Tess lies exhausted on the altar stone, she is arrested and pays the ultimate price in Winchester gaol. *A few minutes after the hour had struck something moved slowly up the staff, and extended itself upon the breeze. It was a black flag.*

William Barnes

William Barnes 1801–1886 was a rural eminent Victorian. Like Thomas Hardy he achieved the unusual distinction amongst country people of gaining national recognition through his poetry, notably his *Poems of Rural Life in the Dorset Dialect* in 1844. Amongst his admirers were Gerard Manley Hopkins who said of him, 'It is as if Dorset life and Dorset language had taken flesh and tongue in the man'.

Barnes was born in the Blackmore Vale two miles west of Sturminster Newton. After his mother's death when he was five he enjoyed a happy childhood in quiet countryside around Pentridge Farm. Many of his poems recollect these years.

The Hwomestead
I'm landlord o' my little farm,
I'm king 'ithin my little pleace;
I don't break laws, an' don't do harm,
An' ben't afeard o' noo man's feace.

One of his favourite activities in later years was to revisit places he had loved in earlier times. His daughters, born to Julia Miles, the love of his life, who he married in 1827, recalled a visit in the 1840s to Ham Hill, which overlooks the Blackmore Vale.

'Towns, and villages, and lonely farmsteads were dotted about, some forming a cluster of warm red or thatched roofs, others only suggested by curling smoke amongst the trees. The poet pointed out each place to his wife. "There was the farm of my grandfather," "that was the house my great-grandfather possessed"; "there was one of my favourite haunts when a boy", and so on, every place seemed to be full of story to him.'

This feeling can be compared with the word pictures from Thomas Hardy's *The Woodlanders* on pages 18 and 19. Similarly in the *Return of the Native* on page 12, Clym probably experiences the same sort of remembrances as William Barnes had after he left the place whose old associations meant so much to him, as they evidently did to Hardy.

From 1827–1835 Barnes lived at the Chantry Houe, Mere, as a schoolmaster. He wrote poetry, enjoyed music and engraved in wood and copper. He read widely, learned more languages and began writing on Philologica a series of letters to *The Dorset County Chronicle* and *The Gentleman's Magazine*.

In the year of the Great Exhibition '1851', the Revd William Barnes's Academy was one of the largest, and potentially best-equipped, schools in Dorset for the sons of the middle-classes. The school declined after the death of William's wife, Julia. In February 1848 he had been ordained at Salisbury. This led to his being offered the living of Winterbourne Came where he lived for the remainder of his life in Came Rectory, which still survives a mile out of Dorchester by the main road to Wareham.

In his old age Barnes became a familiar sight in Dorchester on market days 'quaintly attired in caped cloak, knee breeches and buckled shoes with a leather satchel slung over his shoulder and a short staff in his hand'. He would 'pull his old fashioned watch from its deep fob and set it with great precision to London time'.

William Barnes, the Dorset poet, lived in Came rectory (still visible but not visitable). Hardy described him as 'probably the most interesting link between present and past forms of rural life that England possessed'. He was 'a complete repertory of forgotten manners, words, and sentiments'.

Claire Tomalin, *Thomas Hardy, The Time-Torn Man*, Penguin Viking, 2006

Denys Kay-Robinson, *The Landscape of Thomas Hardy*. Webb & Bower, 1984

Michael Millgate, *Thomas Hardy, A biography*. O.U.P., 1982

F.P. Pitfield, *Hardy's Wessex Locations*, Dorset Publishing Company, 1992

David Wright (ed.), *Thomas Hardy, Selected Poems*. Penguin Books, 1978

Hardy's Cottage at Higher Bockhampton,
  Near Dorchester DT2 8QJ
Max Gate, Alington Avenue, Dorchester DT1 2AB
Dorchester County Museum, Dorchester *are all well worth visiting. The first two are administered by the National Trust.*

WESSEX BOOKS

ROMANS IN WESSEX   *Michael St John Parker*

PREHISTORIC SACRED SITES OF WESSEX   *George Wingfield & Jürgen Krönig*

ALFRED THE GREAT   *Douglas Stuckey*

LABYRINTHS AND MAZES   *Geoffrey Ashe*

STONEHENGE EARTH AND SKY   *Gerald Hawkins*

CROP CIRCLES THE HIDDEN FORM   *Nick Kollerstrom*

SIR CHRISTOPHER WREN   *Michael St John Parker*

IRON AGE CELTS IN WESSEX   *David Allen*